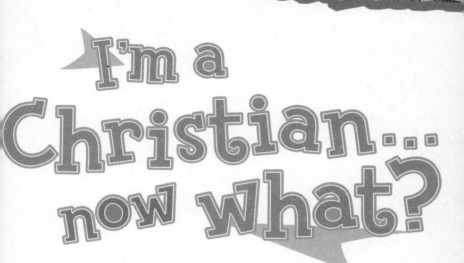

I'm a Christian... now what?

Written by
Jesse Campbell

100 Devotions for Boys

978-1-4336-8566-8

Published by B&H Publishing Group
Nashville, Tennessee

Dewey Decimal Classification: 242.62
Subject Heading: BOYS \ CHRISTIAN LIFE \ DEVOTIONAL
LITERATURE

All Scripture quotations are taken from
the Holman Christian Standard Bible®, Copyright ©
1999, 2000, 2002, 2003, 2009 by Holman Bible Publishers.

1 2 3 4 5 6 • 18 17 16 15

Contents

Introduction

Congratulations on your new relationship with Jesus Christ! My name is Jesse Campbell, and I'm stoked out of my mind for you. I remember what it was like for me when I began my Christian walk a long time ago, and I wish I had a G.P.S. of some sort. That's what I hope this book is for you. We're going to lay the groundwork for your relationship with Christ and build upon what God taught us in my earlier book, *What It Means to Be a Christian*.

So, you're a Christian! Now what? Now this . . .

Our first week will be a crash course on the basics, but after that you will need to make three bookmarks out of sturdy paper. I'll prompt you to write on these bookmarks in an ongoing exercise that will teach you the discipline of Christian journaling. They will also make cool mementos for you decades from now as you look back on these first days of your faith. The first bookmark will be your Matt Marker as it tracks our progress through Matthew. The second will be your Acts Axe as we take a tour through Acts, and the third will be your Leaping Leaflet because it is going to take huge jumps through the Bible each time you use it.

For more stuff just for the readers of this book, visit me at jessethecampbell.com. Click "BOOKS" and then the button for *I'm a Christian—Now What?*

I Am with You Always

MATTHEW 28:18–20

It took a second for the realization to wash over me: I had just seen my friend saved. I'd never put myself out there like that before and the words that came out of my mouth seemed too smart and spiritual for me to have thought up myself. The last part of today's passage immediately came to my mind and that is, "And remember, I am with you always, to the end to the age." Now that you're a Christian, it's time to obey Jesus' final command. Today, we encounter the Great Commission. *Read today's Scripture.*

So, the disciples have now been told to go and make *other* disciples. Those who had been baptized and taught were told to baptize and teach. (By the way, have you been baptized yet?) This Commission applies to you as well! So, you're a Christian? Great, now make other Christians. I'm here to coach you on how to do that. I've written a rap that helps you remember how to share the gospel, and it's available on my website jessethecampbell.com. Click on "BOOKS" and then the button for *this* book. Now, listen to the "EvangeRap."

How can you begin to share your faith?

Have You Been Baptized?

ACTS 2:37–41

I just baptized eleven students this morning! Seriously, my wife, kids, and I just came home from church where I baptized eleven students and then God laid you on my heart, so I went straight to my laptop. Have you been baptized yet? If not, dude, you're missing the first answer to the question, "I'm a Christian—now what?" Now that you're a Christian, just as a group of my newest students did this morning, *get baptized!* In Acts 22:16, Paul says that God asked him, "Why delay? Get up and be baptized." *Read today's Scripture.*

Now, through a phone call, or their website, have your parents or guardians get in touch with a local church that teaches the Bible and learn what their service times are. If you were given this book at a church, then I guess you know which one to call, huh? Speak with someone at the church about scheduling your baptism and then spread the word to your friends and family! Inviting people to your baptism is an awesome way to minister to people. It's the way we officially become church members, and today's text (along with Acts 22:16) tells us to do it right away!

If you've been baptized, write down the date.
If not, write out a plan to get baptized soon.

_____

_____

_____

_____

_____

_____

_____

_____

_____

_____

_____

_____

_____

A Dangerous Habit

HEBREWS 10:23–25

Did you listen to the EvangeRap? If not, with your parent's or guardian's permission, download it to whatever you use to listen to music, or just hit "play." If you get it stuck in your head, you'll have a handy memory trick for the rest of your life in sharing the gospel. The drumming in the EvangeRap, if I say so myself, isn't too shabby! Yep, that's me doing something God called me to do: hit stuff with sticks. Now, in yesterday's text, we saw Peter speak to a crowd about the Holy Spirit. The Holy Spirit is who we receive upon salvation and He is a huge part of worship. Worship is the act of glorifying God and corporate worship, more specifically, is the act of glorifying God alongside other Christians. *Read today's Scripture.*

It's a dangerous habit (verse 25 of today's text) to miss out on worship over and over. We need to worship with other believers because we need to be encouraged by worshipping alongside them *and* we need to worship with other believers in church so that we can encourage them! Encounter the Holy Spirit regularly as a faithful member of a church.

What does being a faithful church member mean to you?

The Bible Is Complete

REVELATION 22:17–21

"I have treasured Your word in my heart so that I may not sin against You." That's Psalm 119:11 in the Holman Christian Standard Bible. Think for a minute about the very words of God in your own heart; Jesus in word form (John 1:1) at the very core of your being. Deep, huh? The Bible that we as evangelical Christians use was inspired by the Holy Spirit of God to messed up earthly men like you and me. Every word of it is breathed by God (2 Timothy 3:16) and it changes everything (Hebrews 4:12). Check out the last words of the Bible. *Read today's Scripture.*

Now that you're a Christian, you need to understand fully just how vitally important your Bible is. It's the best thing you've got going for you! Today's text is its seal. The Bible is complete! Now that you're a Christian, let your heart's prayer be the last sentence of verse 20. That means you want God's plans including His Second Coming more than you want your own. Don't get up from your seat until you've prayed "Amen! Come, Lord Jesus!" with a heart that's honestly submissive to God.

Write out your prayer asking Jesus to come quickly.

_____

_____

_____

_____

_____

_____

_____

_____

_____

_____

_____

_____

_____

_____

Sanctification

ROMANS 8:28–30

As we continue through these 100 days together, I'll be able to tell you more about my testimony (my story as a Christian), but for now I'll tell you that my wife and I know about pain and difficulty. We have a son named Aiden who died and is in heaven. Like verse 28 of today's text says, God used even that difficulty to bring about beautiful and good things. Later in this book, we'll look at the books of James and 1 Peter that teach about suffering. *Read today's Scripture*.

This passage, in verse 30, introduces us to something called "sanctification." Sanctification is the process of God making us like Himself. This process of God stripping away our sin nature will take our whole lives and then, once we are in heaven, we will be glorified with Christ (verses 29–30). Ephesians 5:27 also talks about how we as God's church will be made holy and blameless without a spot. God has always had a plan for you (verse 29) and that plan is to make you like His Son Jesus. As we go through this lifelong process of sanctification, we continually repent from sin.

Write out ways you can strive to be more like Jesus.

_____

_____

_____

_____

_____

_____

_____

_____

_____

_____

_____

_____

_____

_____

_____

Prayer Life

1 THESSALONIANS 5:16–18

Now that you're a Christian, your prayer life can truly begin! You may be unfamiliar with some of the terms you hear used by people at your church who have been saved (Christians) for a long time. For example, "How's your prayer life?" is a way of asking how often or how intensely you pray. Also, "I'm trying to find God's will," means that person is trying to figure out what God would have him do in a certain situation. Today's text brings both of those ideas together beautifully. I'm about to share something I can definitely say is God's will for your life and it has to do with prayer! *Read today's Scripture.*

Should you pray about little things? Yes! Ephesians 6:18 says we should "pray at all times . . . with every prayer and request." Should you pray even when you don't need anything? Yes! Today's text says it is God's will that you would pray *constantly* and give thanks "in everything." Start the rest of your day from this point on in a constant state of prayer, rejoicing and thanking God for everything (verses 16 and 18) and don't say "Amen" until you fall asleep tonight.

Set aside a time every day for prayer. Write it down and commit to it.

Are You Called to Ministry?

2 TIMOTHY 1:1–14

(Today's passage is our longest yet! Buck up!)

Today, I'm a pastor, author, and professional drummer, but for my whole teenage life I was hard core on track to become an electrical engineer. As we close out this opening week-long crash course on what happens now that you're a Christian and prepare to start our three day cycles, I want to introduce an idea that may seem about as obscure to you as the thought of a brown Skittle flavor. I want you to think about the possibility that you might be called to the ministry as your job one day. *Read today's Scripture.*

Now, we are all called to do ministry in some form or another. Here, this young guy named Timothy was prayed over and commissioned (verse 6) to be the pastor of this huge church in the city of Ephesus. Would you pray now about the specifics of God's will for your life? Pray that God would guide you as He guided the dudes in the book of Acts; by the power of His Holy Spirit. Through the Holy Spirit, we don't need to be afraid of God's call on our lives. Instead, we have a spirit of power, love, and sound judgment (verse 7)!

How are you called to do ministry?

_____

_____

_____

_____

_____

_____

_____

_____

_____

_____

_____

_____

_____

_____

_____

_____

_____

_____

Sermon on the Mount

MATTHEW 5:11–20

You are going to be discipled directly by Jesus through the gospel of Matthew as we pick up some of the pieces that were missing from *What It Means to Be a Christian*. Do you know what the word *discipled* means? It means that Jesus is going to teach you how to be a Christian. The fifth chapter of Matthew through much of the seventh contain the famous "Sermon on the Mount." This is the greatest sermon ever preached. *Read today's Scripture.*

In this sermon, Jesus is laying out just how much we need His grace and this is an important thing for Christians to remember. When we start thinking we've got our act together and feeling like we have righteousness on our own—righteousness that gives us any sort of right to tell God what's up—we should just review these first sections of the Sermon on the Mount. The whole thing opens (verses 1–10) with a list of the people who are blessed with a joy that surpasses circumstance. Check it out and see how many of these verses describe you. Also, leave a bookmark that we'll call your Matt Marker at this passage in your Bible.

Write down the things that describe you from Matthew 5.

_____

_____

_____

_____

_____

_____

_____

_____

_____

_____

_____

_____

_____

_____

_____

_____

What Is Happening?

ACTS 1:8–11

Some books of the Bible are historical: they tell us what happened. Apocalyptic books tell us what's going to happen. This book of the Bible, however, tells us what *is happening*. It starts immediately after the events of the Gospels as the resurrected Jesus goes up into heaven. The disciples said, "Okay, we're Christians—now what?" The book of Acts is their *ongoing* answer. Today, we start our survey of Acts. As we hop through, you'll need a good bookmark for the Acts that we'll call your Acts Axe just like you'll need a bookmark for our survey of the passages throughout the book of Matthew. We'll call that bookmark your Matt Marker. Make these bookmarks a pretty good size each and choose a kind of paper that you can write miniature journal entries on. *Read today's Scripture.*

God's presence on the earth began with God the Father in the Garden of Eden (and again on Mt. Sinai). He was in the cloud that guided the Israelites, inhabited the ark of the covenant, was born physically in Jesus, and is now among us as the Holy Spirit since Jesus' Pentecost. Now what, Christian? Now, the Holy Spirit is upon your life.

What does it mean to have the Holy Spirit in your life?

_____

_____

_____

_____

_____

_____

_____

_____

_____

_____

_____

_____

_____

_____

_____

Buff Hairy Gorilla

EXODUS 14:19–22

Yeah, like a heavily caffeinated bandicoot, every third devotional from here through the rest of the book is going to come from a passage selection that jumps seemingly sporadically through the Bible. As a result of your tri-weekly page flipping, you'll become a ninja who is able to find any given passage at a moment's notice. Having the ability to navigate your Bible gives you a buff hairy gorilla-man chest. I promise I have chosen these passages very strategically and prayerfully, so it's worth the extra flipping effort. (Ha! No pun intended.) So, now make a third bookmark on which you can write. This one will be called our Leaping Leaflet because it's a leaflet of paper that leaps through the Bible. *Read today's Scripture.*

According to 1 Corinthians 10:2, this was the nation of Israel's Old Testament-style baptism! Baptism has its roots all the way back in Exodus. God had baptism in mind all along. We see it in the flood (1 Peter 3:18–22), in the Red Sea (today's Scripture), and in the Jordan River (Joshua 3). Can you see how important baptism is to God? If you haven't yet, schedule your baptism today!

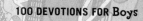

Why do you think baptism is important?

_____

_____

_____

_____

_____

_____

_____

_____

_____

_____

_____

_____

_____

Secret-Agent Style

MATTHEW 6:1–4

Today, someone left an envelope for me with $500 and a card that said, "Thank you for all you do!" This was *such* an epic blessing for me! Now, according to today's text, that person who left the envelope for me is also especially blessed by God because he (the handwriting has vaguely dude-like attributes) did it secret-agent style! *Read today's Scripture.*

So, it's a big deal to God that Christians be people who give, but it's also a big deal to God that we give *in a certain way*. We can't give to someone who is in need and then post it all over the Internet so people will go crazy about what generous guys we are. No, if we do that, we won't be blessed by God because we'll be taking glory for ourselves (verse 2). We should give because giving flows from our hearts. In the upcoming verses 19–21, we learn that the way we spend money shows where our hearts are and that storing up earthly treasures makes no sense compared to storing up heavenly treasures. Now, I want you to secretly give a gift to someone today and write about it on your Matt Marker.

Who did you choose to give a gift to and why?

_____

_____

_____

_____

_____

_____

_____

_____

_____

_____

_____

_____

_____

A Powerful Miracle

ACTS 2:1–13

Read today's Scripture. This is the first of seven outpourings of the Holy Spirit in the book of Acts and it served a special purpose. Because not everyone spoke the same language, this miracle lifted the curse of the tower of Babel where man's speech was confused and allowed the gospel to jump language barriers. Though one man's vocal cords, tongues, teeth, and lips were moving the way they needed to in speaking one language, the foreigner to whom he was speaking *heard* him in his own language! This powerful miracle was a huge leap in communicating the gospel, but it was also a miracle of the Holy Spirit (can you just imagine that wind sound in verse 2 and the flames in verse 3) that convinced countless onlookers (verses 7–12 and 1 Corinthians 14:22). Most of the outpourings of the Holy Spirit in the book of Acts don't involve the gift of tongues, and Paul has some clear instructions on it in 1 Corinthians 14, so we know you don't need to have an experience identical to this one in order to be saved, but being saved and having the Holy Spirit go hand in hand (Romans 8:5–11).

What goes hand in hand with the Holy Spirit?

_____

_____

_____

_____

_____

_____

_____

_____

_____

_____

_____

_____

_____

_____

Putting Our Sin to Death

JOSHUA 3:15–17

Read today's Scripture. I hope you understand what a beautiful thing baptism is. What we just read is not only an awesome teaching on how God carries us through overwhelming things (see our upcoming studies in James and 1 Peter) to the other side where He has a plan for us, but it is also another Old Testament fore-shadowing of baptism. In this passage, it's Joshua's turn to lead the Israelites through what we read about in our last Leaping Leaflet passage.

John the Baptist ("J. to the B." if you read *What It Means to Be a Christian*) baptized people to repent for their sins in preparation for Jesus' arrival. Then, he baptized Jesus (Matthew 3)! In Romans 6:1–11, which is where pastors get their words used in performing a baptism, Paul writes about how baptism is our way of sharing with Christ's burial after the crucifixion. We put our sin to death and don't live in it any longer. Then, we are raised to walk in a new life as we share in Christ's resurrection. That's what is represented when someone is lifted up out of the water in baptism, they're sharing in Jesus' resurrection!

What does baptism represent?

Fasting and Prayer

MATTHEW 6:9–18

Ready, set, back to the Gospel of Matthew! Through these passages, Jesus is discipling us. Today, He's going to teach us how to practice two disciplines. In verses 9–15, He'll show us a prayer that we can use as a model for our own prayers, then He'll teach us how to fast, which means (in this instance) to choose not to eat for spiritual reasons. *Read today's Scripture.*

Fasting and prayer go together because fasting usually is done for a specific prayer-motivated purpose. Every time your stomach growls, you pray for whatever it is that first led you to fast. When you pray, you start with praise for God (verse 9) as that puts everything else in perspective including the rest of your prayer. Then, you submit to God (verse 10), ask for His provisions the way the Israelites did in the desert (verse 11), and then ask for His deliverance from temptation and evil (verse 13). Now, it's time to try this awesome ancient discipline of our faith that has been practiced by awesome men of God for many years. With your parents' permission and even participation, fast for a few hours drinking only water and praying.

What are your prayer requests during your fast?

_____

_____

_____

_____

_____

_____

_____

_____

_____

_____

_____

_____

_____

_____

Standing Like Peter

ACTS 2:14–15

I once taught a series entitled "Origins" highlighting the miracles of the book of Acts. *Read today's Scripture.*

Ha! I love this passage. Now, to fully appreciate what a big deal it is for Peter to stand up and address the crowd, you have to understand Peter's story. He swore he would stand by Jesus until death, and then, as the crucifixion started to go down, Peter ran off and then swore three times that he didn't even know Jesus. It was humiliating and Jesus prophesied that it would happen. So, Peter let Jesus down when things got tough. We'll talk more about that on Day 28. (It's okay. Go ahead and peek. I won't tell.) Today, however, we see Peter completely transformed! He went from cowering at the accusations of a servant girl and sobbing about it (Matthew 26:69–75) to raising his voice at a crowd and leading thousands of people to Christ (verses 14 and 41)! Write on your Acts Axe bookmark what it would mean for you to stand up to the crowd like Peter did in today's text.

What would it mean for you to stand up to a crowd?

_____

_____

_____

_____

_____

_____

_____

_____

_____

_____

_____

_____

_____

Be Strong and Courageous

JOSHUA 1:5–9

In my office, there's a sword mounted on my wall. I'm serious. It has an old-school cross on the handle. My dad gave it to me the day I was ordained and commissioned for ministry. That was a really cool mountain top in my journey through manhood . . . plus, it comes in handy when bad guy ninjas bust through the office window. Now that you're a Christian, it's time to be captivated by the vision of yourself as a Christian *man*. Joshua was an awesome man of God. *Read today's Scripture.*

In my book *365 Devos for Teen Guys*, we look pretty in depth at this, but today's passage gives a cool introduction to the idea. Joshua is told over and over to be strong and courageous. Like my ordination ceremony where I received the sword from my dad, Joshua is receiving this powerful anointing from God to carry on the work of Moses. He's told over and over to be strong and courageous and right now, I'm telling you to be strong and courageous because God is with you wherever you go (verse 9)!

What can you do to stand strong and courageous?

_____

_____

_____

_____

_____

_____

_____

_____

_____

_____

_____

_____

_____

_____

Stop It

MATTHEW 6:24–34

Don't worry. You're worrying, man. Stop it. Chill. God is always good even when life isn't. God is going to get you through this. Don't obsess over money and worldly possessions and don't let a lack of them stress you out. Don't be afraid of tomorrow. Just focus on today. Now, *read today's Scripture.*

Don't you know how much you are worth to God? Seek Him first above everything else and everything else will fall into place (verse 33). Philippians 4:6–7 tells us not to worry about anything, but to tell God with thankful hearts everything we need and then the peace of God that surpasses every thought will guard your heart and mind in Christ Jesus. This will be a constant struggle now that you're a Christian, but keeping Christ at the top of your priorities will help you remember how much bigger God is than all the things that worry you. Write on your Matt Marker this covenant to your future self, "I will put God first and, as a result, I won't worry so much." Now, listen to and sing Third Day's song, "It's Alright."

Write out the chorus from the song "It's Alright."

_____

_____

_____

_____

_____

_____

_____

_____

_____

_____

_____

_____

Walking and Leaping

ACTS 3:19

After Peter speaks that message at Pentecost and the Holy Spirit comes in power, he and John heal a man in the name of Jesus Christ of Nazareth (the town Jesus came from after being born in Bethlehem and a quick stay in Egypt when He was little). The man went from paralyzed to "walking and leaping, and praising God" (verse 8), all over the temple courts. This, obviously, caused a big stir and today's passage comes from Peter's response to the unbelieving crowd that is looking on. *Read today's Scripture.*

Are you in a dry time in your walk with God right now? Is the "newness" of your faith starting to wear off a bit? That's okay. It happens and being able to stay true to your faith in Jesus, even when you don't feel like it, is part of becoming mature. Peter's words to these unbelievers is equally true to believers whose walks with God are dry. Repent from sin and turn back to God so that a time of refreshing may come from God! On your Acts Axe, write down a code word for a sin that has been kicking your tail. Repent and be refreshed.

What's your code word? Now pray and ask for help with it.

_____

_____

_____

_____

_____

_____

_____

_____

_____

_____

_____

_____

_____

_____

Getting Muddy in the Pit

1 SAMUEL 17:31–51

Did you repent from that sin? Did you experience that refreshment spiritually that repentance brings? Dude, it's like a shower after a mud fight. My students and I just had another huge mud war. Students went back and forth between getting muddy in the pit and getting cleaned off on the massive slip & slide. It was one big messy teaching illustration. *Read today's Scripture.*

After forty days of hearing Goliath come forward and mock the army of the Living God, little David has had enough. He was fearless! He took on this giant in the name of Yahweh (God) and did it to prove God to those looking on (verses 45–47). David was man of godly might and that's what I want you to be. I want you to see the giants in your life and remember that your God is bigger. Like David, I want you to be the kind of man who doesn't just take on the giant, but the crowd of suck-ups behind him. Let no giant and no crowd (talking about your classmates, neighbors, teammates, or even buddies) intimidate you. Live out your faith publicly.

How can you live out your faith?

Bring in the Harvest

MATTHEW 9:35–38

Read today's Scripture. Did you see how Jesus felt about His crowd of lost people? Did you see how He looks at the lost and feels compassion for them? Let that teach you much about the nature of God. Let it reveal to you a part of His heart. This is how Jesus feels about the lost people in your life. He sees them and their diseases (verse 35). He sees their weariness and their complete lack of guidance (verse 36). Outside of a Christian worldview, there is no solid sense of morality. It's hard to tell what's right from what's wrong sometimes and it's impossible to find a truly eternal sense of purpose to life. This is the majority of the human race, Christian. Most of humanity is lost and there are not enough Christians working to bring in the harvest. May you be a worker who evangelizes and brings in the harvest!

Right now, write a commitment on your Matt Marker that you will be a worker in this abundant harvest! Include today's date. As you do, know that I am going to ask you later to revisit it to see if you follow through.

What's your commitment to help bring in the harvest?

_____

_____

_____

_____

_____

_____

_____

_____

_____

_____

_____

_____

_____

_____

_____

Owning Your Identity

ACTS 4:1–4

What if you blow it? I mean, what if you go for it evangelistically, go for it as a publicly loud testimony for Christ, and then just royally mess the whole thing up? What if you put yourself out there fully owning your identity as a Christian and then, right there in that public arena with all the lost looking on, things don't go according to plan and you stumble? In today's text, Peter and John are out there teaching people that Jesus rose again from the dead, and then they're arrested. They're shut down. Game over. Go home. All hope is lost, right? Nope. *Read today's Scripture.*

Look at that! I think that being put in jail unjustly is about the worst case scenario and it's exactly what happens, but five thousand people were saved anyway! It was the same thing when Peter messed up and lost faith walking on the water to Jesus. People watching from the boat were saved anyway!

What caused Peter to mess up?

_____

_____

_____

_____

_____

_____

_____

_____

_____

_____

_____

_____

_____

_____

_____

_____

A Vision on the Horizon

SONG OF SONGS 1:15–17

Today, I'm going to introduce you to a truly unique book of the Bible. It's this conversation between Solomon and his bride, and it includes input from their friends. *Read today's Scripture.*

This man knows how to talk to a woman. He should. He was given the gift of superior wisdom by God (1 Kings 3:13). Look at how she reflects his feelings in verse 16. I want you to think about marriage and I want you to have a vision on the horizon of your life to one day hear your wife speak to you the way this woman did to Solomon—with admiration and respect. In all of your dealings with women today, I want you to be especially respectful. Leave no chair pushed in, or door unopened as a woman approaches. Write on your Leaping Leaflet that you will be marriage minded in the way you treat women.

In what ways can you be respectful of girls and women?

_____

_____

_____

_____

_____

_____

_____

_____

_____

_____

_____

_____

_____

_____

A Clueless Christian

MATTHEW 10:1–16

Read today's Scripture. Memorize verse 16. Jesus just told His disciples He was putting them in harm's way. Did you know that God's will is not actually the safest place to be? Did you know that it is not actually a good thing to be a clueless Christian? As a Christian, you have been sent out like a sheep among wolves. Colossians 4:5 tells us to "act wisely toward outsiders, making the most of the time." You're going to be rejected and outnumbered by people whose lives may be hostile to the gospel. This is God's will for many of you. This is what following the Great Commission often looks like.

Jesus tells the apostles (the sent-out ones) that towns that reject their message do so at their own peril (verse 15). Those who reject the gospel will answer to God for it. The stakes are high and the opposition can be hateful, so be wise. Know how you're perceived. Know when someone is just trying to get a rouse out of you and don't waste time "tossing your pearls before pigs" (Matthew 7:6), but be as shrewd as a serpent while keeping your integrity intact.

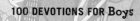

What can you do to keep your integrity intact?

_____

_____

_____

_____

_____

_____

_____

_____

_____

_____

_____

_____

_____

_____

The Great Commission

ACTS 4:23–31

Peter and John are released from prison, pray to God for boldness, and then go right back at it; evangelizing even more. Their prayer is one God will always answer in the affirmative. They're automatically praying in accordance with the will of God because they're asking God for the boldness to fulfill the Great Commission, and the Great Commission is obviously God's will because God commands it! *Read today's Scripture.*

In prayer, they bring before God the threats they've faced. Would you do that right now? Then, they pray for boldness. Would you do that now? After this prayer, the building they're in is literally shaken! They were filled with the Holy Spirit and anytime people in the book of Acts are filled with the Holy Spirit, something *awesome* happens. It's not like, "they were filled with the Holy Spirit and then played Scrabble and Peter won 72 points with the word *fungus*." No! The miracles of Acts are always preceded with the apostles praying, worshipping in some form, and being filled with the Holy Spirit! Give God thanks, and then ask Him for boldness to proclaim the truth and for the guidance of the Holy Spirit (see Luke 11:13 and Colossians 4:2–4).

Write a prayer of thanks to God.

_____

_____

_____

_____

_____

_____

_____

_____

_____

_____

_____

_____

_____

The Megalodon

PROVERBS 1:1–7

We've met Solomon who was given superior wisdom by God, and we're going to see that superior God-given wisdom applied *directly* to you and your life right now. The books of Psalms and Proverbs are called the "wisdom and poetry" books. Proverbs is expressly written for young men like you! Solomon writes most of it and we go through every single amazing word in my book 365 *Devos for Teen Guys. Read today's Scripture.*

The man of superior wisdom tells us precisely where wisdom begins. It begins by fearing the Lord (verse 7). Now, this is not fear the way I fear that the prehistoric bus-sized shark known as the *megalodon* still exists, knows my name, and is coming for me each time I go surfing. It's fear in the sense that you understand God to be all-powerful, perfectly holy, and beautifully dangerous. It makes perfect sense because all the wisdom of the world flows from this. Like Solomon says, it's step one. This is what we call a *worldview*. Atheists (people who don't believe in God) have no step one. We, however, know where the universe came from and so our wisdom begins.

What is step one for gaining wisdom?

Speaking of Repetition

MATTHEW 10:16–20

I'll never forget the time I first debated with an atheist. He was way smarter than me. He knew his stuff better than I knew mine. Yet, what little I knew was used by God to make an impact on him, that was indelible (a big deal). Now that you're a Christian you have the Holy Spirit of God within you. *Read today's Scripture.*

I know this passage overlaps with our last glimpse into Matthew's gospel, but verse 16 is just so important for you right now that it's worth repeating even more than these two times. Speaking of repetition (speaking of repetition), read verse 20 again! Whoa! The Holy Spirit of our heavenly Father gives us words when we're speaking to the "opposition" (verse 19). So, that explains why I have seen men smarter than me silenced at what I have answered or asked: the Holy Spirit of God gave me wisdom at those times. My student, be emboldened because you have been empowered, empowered by the Holy Spirit of God who speaks through Christians in their times of need! Write what's on your heart right now onto your Matt Marker. You might need it later.

What's on your heart today?

Tithes

ACTS 5:1–16

You're going to tithe. Yes, you. You are going to bring a "donation" to your church this coming weekend and, in so doing, you are going to experience the powerful act of proving your heart's alignment with the things of God (Luke 12:34). By giving even part of your treasure to the Lord, your heart is shown to belong to God. Giving with a grateful and joyful heart (2 Corinthians 9:7), you are going to experience perhaps a new way to worship God. Let liars' hearts be terrified as you *read today's Scripture.*

So, it's obviously not enough just to give something to the church (I hope you'd be sadly amazed how many Christians give *nothing*), but you must also give *authentically*. Now, notice the degree of fear (verses 11 and 13) that was associated with the burgeoning (blossoming) original New Testament church. We like to look only at Acts 2 and see what was essentially a commune in which people shared everything and say, "Wow, what a nice pretty time of unicorns and butterflies," but it was also a time marked with fear as sinful people came to know their own holy God. This weekend, authentically give.

What does giving authentically mean to you?

Foundation of the Unconquerable Church

JOHN 21:15–19

Now that you're a Christian, it's time to give. Did you give, or have you truly planned to give as you were so challenged yesterday? We covered the passage preceding this one in *What It Means to Be a Christian*. Jesus told Peter that his profession of faith would be the foundation for God's unconquerable church (Matthew 16:18). Peter publicly denied knowing Jesus three times during Jesus' trial just as Jesus prophesied he would (Matthew 26:74–75), and we are now wondering what the resurrected Jesus said to Peter. So, with a passage that may seem to come out of nowhere, *read today's text.*

There will be times that you as a Christian let Christ down. However, look at the direct, perfect, and even painful way in which Jesus ministers healing to Peter in this text. What a merciful God we love. Even after our failures, He restores and heals us! If God used Peter to lead about 3,000 people to Christ (Acts 2:41) even after Peter completely ditched Jesus (Matthew 26:69–75), just imagine what God can do through you. Even after periods of doubt, God can still use you to achieve powerful things that change others' lives!

What powerful things can you do?

_____

_____

_____

_____

_____

_____

_____

_____

_____

_____

_____

_____

_____

_____

_____

_____

Rest

MATTHEW 12:1–8

Read today's Scripture. We were programmed with the rhythm of God's pace in creating the world. Yes, I believe in the Genesis seven-day creation. This innate sense of resting every seventh day was echoed in the Ten Commandments and resonates today. I believe that God's fourth commandment (Exodus 20:8) to rest every seventh day still applies, but I see in the New Testament epistles (letters) that the day upon which you take this rest to honor God (Mark 2:27) is up to your personal convictions (Colossians 2:16–17). So, if you're doing ministry work on your Sabbath day, then take another day to rest. Jesus did a great deal of ministry and healing on the Sabbath, but He was also Lord over the Sabbath (Matthew 12:8).

I want you to look up and download a song by a band that I both love and have drummed for (though I doubt they remember me) called Big Daddy Weave. Back when I filled in for their drummer on that one gig, they were basically still called Big Daddy Weave and the Institution. Look up "Rest" by Big Daddy Weave and worship in Sabbath rest, Christian.

How will you rest on the Sabbath?

Personal Discipleship

ACTS 5:17–21

Of the atheists I've seen come to salvation by the power of the Holy Spirit, one who is particularly special to my heart came to my ministry regularly over the course of about a year before being saved. After a season of personal discipleship, this *former* atheist was called by God into ministry! This came in part from God's call on my heart to share my life. The most fruitful season of my life evangelistically so far came when I opened up my story to my church and the world about our son Aiden and praying the impossible for him. It increased even more after that as I opened up to the world about my grief after his death. In all of this, I was telling the world about this life walking with Christ resolute that I will trust God no matter what. *Read today's Scripture.*

The false converts (people who claimed to be Christians but did not do the will of God) tried to shut them up, but they just kept teaching about their life with Christ and people kept being saved. Write on your Acts Axe a commitment to tell others about this life with Christ!

What is your commitment to tell others about Christ?

_____

_____

_____

_____

_____

_____

_____

_____

_____

_____

_____

_____

_____

_____

_____

Encountering God

ROMANS 1:1–25

Today, we will read from the first chapter of one of the most theologically (*theology* is the study of God) deep books of the Bible right up there with Ephesians and Revelation. This opening chapter along with the next chapter we'll look at will change your life forever if you get them. Have you ever wondered about that person who never hears about the gospel of Jesus and then spends eternity apart from God? *Read today's Scripture.*

According to verses 18–20, every person on this planet has, to some degree, encountered God's existence and God's nature. So, there is no one who will have an excuse before God in judgment (verse 20). When people who have, by their own consciences, been shown the truth of God, their hearts are either deceived like the heart represented by the soil of Jesus' parable in Matthew 13:4 and 13:7, hard like the heart described in Matthew 13:5–6, or receptive like the heart described in Matthew 13:8. Did you know that the word *conscience* is a combination of a word meaning "with" (con-) and word meaning "knowledge" (-science)? So, we all *know* God's law and violate it still!

What excuses do you use in your daily life?

Seriously Do It!

MATTHEW 12:22–32

Alright, this passage is going to be difficult, but I know that you're up to the challenge! Do some stretches, some push-ups, and scowl into the mirror and roar. Seriously do it. You done? Okay, I'm going to define two "b" words for you, so that you'll understand them when you see them. "Beelzebul" is another name for Satan. "Blasphemy" is the act of hating the Holy Spirit and calling Him evil. You've got this! Ready? *Read today's Scripture!*

Whew! You alright? This is the sin that will not be forgiven because the person who commits it will not repent from it: the person who commits blasphemy is an unsaved person who will remain unsaved. This person has some really messed up beliefs and is hard-hearted like the false teachers of 1 Timothy 4:2. Though you may not typically look up these passages in parenthesis, I want you to look up Acts 7:51 wherein Stephen tells the angry Jewish mob who is about to kill him (seriously) that they and their forefathers always resisted the Holy Spirit. As we introduce Romans, this biblically recorded capacity and history of man is important.

Write your thoughts on today's Scripture.

There Is Still Hope

ACTS 5:33–42

Paul, once called "Saul," was formerly the one-on-one student of the greatest teacher in all the Jewish community. (Jewish teachers are called "rabbis" as in *rab-eyes*.) Paul's teacher was named Gamaliel (gahm-Ay-lee-ehl), and Gamaliel was one of the oldest and most respected rabbis of his day (verse 34). He was one of those few men who didn't speak often, but when he did, every other brilliant and accomplished man in the room immediately shut up. Paul, even after his conversion (which is still yet-to-come as of this chapter), was proud to be Gamaliel's private student (Acts 22:3). *Read today's Scripture.*

Gamaliel, though we never see him recorded in the Bible as a converted Christian, had it right in this passage. There's a chance he became a believer in Jesus, a Messianic Jew (say *Mess-see-an-ick*), a believer who still practices some Jewish traditions. In *What It Means to Be a Christian*, we covered *several* prophecies from the Old Testament describing the Messiah, prophecies that are perfectly fulfilled in Jesus in the New Testament. That person in your life who seems like he's too far away from Christ, like Gamaliel, still has hope to be saved!

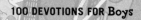

What is a Messianic Jew?

Evangelism Is Necessary

ROMANS 10:10–17

Wow, what an important passage. Seriously, if you read only one devotional in this book, I hope it's this one. *Read today's Scripture.*

Read these words carefully: evangelism is necessary. There are life-changing implications to that. Some Christians are bewildered and even shaken to the core of their weak faith by the question "How could God allow someone who has never heard the gospel to go to hell?" But you are going to understand this passage, and it's going to change your life because you understand it. *Because people need to hear the gospel in order to be saved (verses 14–17), you are going to make it your life's purpose to share the gospel.* What could possibly be more important? You read this passage and are overwhelmed by it, and/or you read this passage and it becomes your life's purpose!

How can you share the gospel with your friends?

Dead or Alive?

MATTHEW 12:33–37

Today, I heard from a former student who was deeply broken over the hurtfully sinful behavior of his friend who claimed to be a Christian. We looked at the fruit of his life and didn't see the fruit of a Christian. If you see a tree covered with figs, that thing is a fig tree. If a person's life is filled with Christian fruit, that person's a Christian. If you see a person's life filled with sin and worldliness, there's a good chance that person isn't saved. *Read today's Scripture.*

So, what kind of fruit is flowing from your life? Is it Christian fruit? Your life's fruit indicates what's going on in your heart. So, are you tithing to your church (Matthew 6:21)? Are you bearing fruit that comes from the Holy Spirit (Galatians 5:22–25)? Write on your Matt Marker that you will be a fruit inspector, that you will begin by inspecting the fruit of your own life, and that from that fruit (or lack of fruit), you will see your own Christian life for what it is. Are you dead or alive? Are you saved or lost?

What kind of fruit are you providing?

_____

_____

_____

_____

_____

_____

_____

_____

_____

_____

_____

_____

_____

_____

_____

Get Back to the Basics

ACTS 6:1–7

So, fruit inspector, what did your investigation conclude? If it came up negative or even inconclusive, get back to the basics of the gospel and determine now whether or not Jesus is Lord of your life at all. If you believe in your heart that God raised Him from the dead and you have made Him Lord of your life, then you will be saved (Romans 10:9), but if you haven't, you are in danger of being a Matthew 7:21–23 "Christian." *Read today's Scripture.*

It's not your pastor's job to do the work of ministry. Yes, yes, I know that sounds crazy to someone at a non-growing church of a comparatively small-to-moderate size, but it's scripturally true: the work of a pastor is not to *do the work*, but to *equip YOU to do the work of ministry* (Ephesians 4:11–12). If your pastor does all the work, then one person's doing all the work. If the people of your church do the work under your pastor's guidance, then that's your pastor's ministry *multiplied by the number of people in your church* doing the work! Which church model seems more biblical and therefore effective to you?

Which church model seems to work better?

Will God Call You?

1 CORINTHIANS 14:1–40

(A new record-length devotional)

I spoke with my buddy who is planting a church in Tampa, Florida, about the nature of my Baptist church as opposed to that of his home church that is of another denomination. He grew up in a church that definitely bore fruit for God's kingdom but also did some stuff that was out of line with today's Scripture. He was convicted by today's passage and God used it to call him to plant a new church! How cool is that? Maybe God will call you, too, through *today's Scripture.*

This is how the church should look during worship according to authoritative Scripture. This is what the church ought to be, and we're seeing it become that as we read through the book of Acts. Biblical worship is to be both spirit-filled and orderly (verse 40). Describe on your Leaping Leaflet a worship service that is both filled with the Holy Spirit and orderly in such a way that nonbelievers would be a part of it without saying that Christians are whackos (verse 23 and Colossians 4:5).

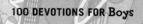

Describe your worship service.

_____

_____

_____

_____

_____

_____

_____

_____

_____

_____

_____

_____

_____

_____

Commit to Be Counted

MATTHEW 13:1–9

Read today's Scripture. Jesus spoke in parables so true Christians would get it and false Christians, who were just faking it, wouldn't get it. Truly converted and therefore fruitful Christians (Romans 8) were those who "had ears" (verse 9). If you read today's passage and didn't get it, I would consider that the most massive red flag of my existence and go straight back to Romans 10:9 before reading on.

Are you about the work of your Savior? Since your conversion experience, have you been about the work of God? If you haven't, you aren't yet saved (Luke 9:62)! So, as a converted and therefore fruitful Christian, go about the work of sowing the seed of the gospel in people's hearts. Go about the work of the Great Commission where this book began. Go about evangelizing. Some will receive it and some won't. On Day 20, you wrote on your Matt Marker a commitment to be counted as a worker in this abundant harvest. Go back to that entry on your Matt Marker and write "Follow up: as of (today's date) I (have or have not) been a worker so far."

How have you been a worker?

_____

_____

_____

_____

_____

_____

_____

_____

_____

_____

_____

_____

_____

_____

_____

Enslaved by the Law

ACTS 6:8–15

Read today's Scripture. If you've been looking up the Scripture references I've given you in parenthesis, then you've already seen what becomes of Stephen here in today's Scripture. He's about to be killed by those to whom he is speaking. The group of men who killed him even had this name that sounds like it would have been an awesome group. It was called the "Freedmen's Synagogue." Yet, these men who proclaimed themselves "free" were enslaved to the law (Galatians 3:1–14). Though they claimed to be worshippers of Yahweh, they didn't recognize Yahweh as He stood right in front of them in the flesh of Jesus (John 14:6–7).

So, in the tradition of Stephen, I want you to proclaim the gospel to those who don't believe.

How can you proclaim the gospel?

_____

_____

_____

_____

_____

_____

_____

_____

_____

_____

_____

_____

_____

_____

Difficulty and Trial

2 CORINTHIANS 12:5–10

My darkest moments as a father weeping over his son's grave have been used to lead countless people to Christ. God uses our weakest moments to demonstrate His strength. In opening this amazing book of 2 Corinthians, Paul says the church of Corinth is his reason for pride as a church planter (2 Corinthians 1:14). A study of this passage was promised in *What It Means to Be a Christian* and is delivered here! *Read today's Scripture.*

Paul was given by God a "thorn in the flesh." Think about that for a moment. Yes, perfect gifts come from God (James 1:17), but sometimes God also brings difficulty and trial. Sometimes, God sabotages us in order to humble us and to teach us. *Do you hear me, my student?* Sometimes, God opposes you for your own good (Haggai 1:5–11)! Yes, because God loves us, He sometimes *opposes* us. Take a minute to fully appreciate that. Then, when you get it, praise God because those weaknesses of yours become the platforms upon which God demonstrates His perfection to the world! He uses your former sins as *weapons* in His war against sin (Romans 6:13—*look it up!*).

What weakness of yours can become a platform?

_____

_____

_____

_____

_____

_____

_____

_____

_____

_____

_____

_____

_____

_____

Wheat and Weeds

MATTHEW 13:18–30

Now that you're a Christian, understand that some people simply won't understand what you say to them when you speak on the Holy Spirit's behalf. Apart from the Holy Spirit of God, they are still stuck in sin and cannot obey God's law until the Holy Spirit draws upon them (Romans 8:7). Knowing this truth will keep you from being discouraged as you evangelize. *Read today's Scripture.*

The opening verses of the passage are an explanation of the last passage we looked at in Matthew. Here, Jesus reveals that those who are deceived by Satan can't understand the gospel (verse 19), those who are super hyped about the gospel at first, but are swept away at the first sign of difficulty aren't saved (verses 20–21), and the one swept away by all the false teachings and a love of wealth can't be saved until he's shown the truth (verse 22 and Luke 18:18–25). Jesus delivers the parable of the Wheat and the Weeds in today's Scripture (verses 24–30) and will explain it in verses 36–43. It paints a picture that's ugly, but realistic. My student, most of the world won't be saved (Matthew 7:13–14).

What do the weeds symbolize in this parable?

A True Martyr

ACTS 7:51–60

Understanding what happens here is crucial to understanding Romans chapters 8–11. Stephen is speaking to Jewish authorities who are resisting the Holy Spirit just like their forefathers did (verse 51). Do you remember our teaching on blasphemy on Day 32? Go back and review if you need to before you *read today's Scripture.*

This is the first time that someone is martyred (killed for his faith) in the New Testament. Stephen gets a standing ovation from God. As he dies, as the stones fatally strike his body, he is praying for the ones throwing them. He is praying for his own executioners. Now, that's a Christian! He gets a standing ovation from Jesus (verse 55) as he is killed by these blasphemers (verse 51) who, like their fathers, resist the Holy Spirit's draw to believe and be saved. Let your heart toward those who persecute you, mock you, and throw stones at you be like that of Stephen in verse 60. Now that you're a Christian, it's time to be like Stephen. Draw a picture on your Acts Axe of Stephen's last moments as described here. Then, meditate on that picture.

Who are today's Christian martyrs?

_____

_____

_____

_____

_____

_____

_____

_____

_____

_____

_____

_____

_____

Inherited Sin

GALATIANS 5:16–26

Did you meditate on your picture of Stephen's martyrdom? I hope so. It's alright if your artwork isn't that good. Mine isn't either. Just ask my family. I hand-painted Valentines for each of them this year and none of them turned out well. As we continue to see what it means to be filled with the Holy Spirit, let's look at the Bible's most straight-forward passage on what comes out of your life when the Holy Spirit comes into it. *Read today's Scripture.*

So, verses 19–21 show us what comes naturally from us as people who have inherited the sin nature and verses 22–26 show us what comes *un*naturally from us as Christians who are filled with the Holy Spirit. God shows us what ought to be and we either believe or disbelieve. When we believe, the attributes described in verses 22–26 flow from us through the Holy Spirit's indwelling. Please don't think of each attribute as a singular fruit, but think of all the fruits combined as "the fruit" as described in verse 22. Because you have love that flows from the Holy Spirit, you're also going to have joy and because you have joy, you'll have peace, etc.

List the fruits of the Spirit. Which are evident in your life?

Running through the Church

MATTHEW 13:54–58

The first church I worked at was the church where I was baptized as a little kid. Though I was voted in, hired, and ordained as a pastor there, some of the adults of the church still remembered this little kid named Jesse who used to run full-speed through the Fellowship Hall during Wednesday night dinner screaming at the top of his lungs. So, as you can imagine, there were some people who had a hard time taking me seriously when I got up in front of them twenty-plus years later to call them out by the power of the Holy Spirit on their sin. *Read today's Scripture.*

Jesus' own half-brothers (half because Jesus wasn't Joseph's biological son) didn't believe in Jesus at first, yet eventually did. Wouldn't it be a miracle if your siblings came to believe you were God? That's what happened with Jesus' half-brothers as they not only came to believe, but became leaders of the early church. James (author of the book of James) became the leader of Jerusalem's church. Now, did you also notice that Jesus would have done more miracles there had the people believed (verse 58)? Meditate on that now.

What do you think Jesus' half-brothers thought about Him?

You Have an Enemy

ACTS 8:1–8

The last time we were with our Acts Axe, Stephen was put to death as the New Covenant's first martyr. Overseeing the execution was this guy named Saul. The funny thing about this guy named Saul is that he would eventually come to be known as "Paul." Now, Paul is the author of much of the New Testament! *Read today's Scripture.*

Now that you're a Christian, you have an enemy. Does that bless you? Isn't that uplifting news? Ha! You see, because you've aligned yourself *with* God, you've aligned yourself *against* Satan. Now, Satan tried to squash the gospel in our last visit to the book of Acts, but as you can see in verse 4, his efforts backfired and the gospel just spread even faster to new places! This backs up Romans 8:28 that teaches us that God uses *all* things for those who are called according to His purpose. Because of Stephen's execution, the gospel spread. People were both exposed to the gospel (verse 4), delivered from demonic possession, and even miraculously healed (verse 7)! Look at and meditate upon the beautiful things that God achieved through Stephen's execution.

How did God still work through Stephen's execution?

_____

_____

_____

_____

_____

_____

_____

_____

_____

_____

_____

_____

_____

_____

_____

_____

_____

Love and Respect

EPHESIANS 5:22–33

My wife lets me know what she thinks, then she follows my lead even if it's in a direction with which she doesn't agree. That's what godly submission looks like for a Christian wife. She speaks everything, *and I mean positively everything* that's on her mind and calls me out when I need to be called out, but still goes along with what I decide. She knows I am accountable to God for how I lead our family and she is accountable to God for how she submits to me. In return, I give my precious bride my very life and consider my every breath meaningless unless it is breathed to love her. *Read today's Scripture.*

We've seen God's design for the church and today we see God's design for the family. God desires that husbands love their wives self-sacrificially, that wives love their husbands respectfully, and that children obey their parents (Ephesians 6:1–3). Take a minute to imagine your future family. Does your wife respect you? Do your children obey you? Now, back to present day, *do you obey your parents as Scripture commands?* Oooooh! Yep, I just went there! BaBam!

How can you show your parents and siblings respect today?

A Massive Meal

MATTHEW 14:13–21

My Student Ministry students sometimes just chuckle at me when I talk about Jesus and food because I teach on the idea pretty frequently, but it's true: food is a big deal to God! Jesus uses food illustrations in His teaching ministry and all Christians will be reunited with God over a *massive* meal (Matthew 26:29). *Read today's Scripture.*

Jesus feeds a huge crowd of people *again* in Matthew 15:32–39 and then uses these mass feasts as a teaching tool in Matthew 16:1–12. Check those passages out for more examples of Jesus teaching through food. For today's passage, however, I want you to see that Jesus takes just five loaves of bread and two fish (verse 19) and *multiplies* them. Did you know that God is still in the business of taking ordinary things and multiplying their impact beyond the possible? God can take all that you are, all that you've been, and all that you're capable of and *multiply* them to achieve things beyond what you can imagine (Ephesians 3:20–21). Write these words on your Matt Marker, "What I can do by myself is nothing compared to what God can do through me."

How has God used others to impact your life?

Saul or Paul

ACTS 9:1–19

Paul has an insane testimony. It's famous because it's dramatic and it's recorded in the Bible, but did you know that even "normal" testimonies are just as powerful as "dramatic" testimonies? When we last saw him, his name was still "Saul" and he was there heartlessly overseeing and approving of Stephen's wrongful execution at the hands of blasphemers in Acts 7. After that, he encountered a powerful manifestation of the resurrected Jesus. He was on his way to the city of Damascus to arrest believers, but things turned out quite differently than he planned. Encountering Jesus tends to have that effect. Instead, he arrived at Damascus blind, believing, and born again. *Read today's Scripture.*

Saul (who would later be renamed "Paul") couldn't see until a believer laid his hand on him and called him "brother" (verse 17). It was horrifying for Ananias to even be near Saul (verse 13), but Ananias obeyed God's call to reach out anyway. Then, Saul received the Holy Spirit (verse 17). Similarly, you have been called to reach out to that person whom you believe is the least likely of all to be saved. Reach out to Saul, Ananias. God has mind-blowing plans for him.

How did being blinded change Saul's faith?

Shine

PHILIPPIANS 2:12–18

I saw her smile. It was a fleeting flash, but I knew that I had seen it. For the first time in a year, I saw my bride's smile again. It wasn't her cordial smile with which she so lovingly and frequently greeted people, but the smile came over her face as joy welled up from within her soul and overflowed to the surface. For the first time since our son, Aiden died, I saw her smile and that was about nine months ago. She smiles everyday now and there was a time we didn't think we could feel joy like this again. *Read today's Scripture.*

The book of Philippians is about joy from beginning to end and is invigorating when you realize that Paul is in prison and facing a death sentence as he writes it. *That* is joy. It's the beautiful sense of eternal purpose that comes from a heavenward focus and the unshakable sense of security that comes from a clear conscience before God and man. This kind of joy cannot be taken away by circumstance. Know that you are saved (verse 12), never complain (verse 14), and hold firmly to the message of life (verse 16). Shine.

What does joy mean to you?

_____

_____

_____

_____

_____

_____

_____

_____

_____

_____

_____

_____

_____

_____

_____

Worship?

MATTHEW 15:1–20

At this point in Matthew, the Pharisees have been plotting for a long time on how they're going to kill Jesus (Matthew 12:14). That is outright wickedness, yet they call Jesus and His disciples out for not washing their hands . . . seriously. *Read today's Scripture.*

Did you catch that prophecy from Isaiah in verses 8–9? Now, be real for a moment. Does that describe you? "These people honor Me with their lips, but their heart is far from Me." Like the shallow group of Old Testament believers whom the prophet Amos called out for their empty worship and prayers recited only from memory, these Pharisees' hearts were not in it. They went through the motions and looked good on the outside, but that was it. When you sing worship songs at church, do you just mouth the words, but your heart is not engaged with the Holy Spirit? If so, you're guilty of the same things for which Jesus calls out the Pharisees here. Honor God not only with your lips, but with your heart as well! Worship in spirit and in truth (John 4:23–24). The next time you're in a worship service, keep this passage in mind, Christian!

How can you honor God in worship?

The Right Questions

ACTS 10:1–6

Sometimes, the hardest part of evangelizing someone is just bringing up the gospel. Here are some questions you can ask that will bring the discussion in that direction. Depending on what you already know about this person, you can ask, "When you go to church, where do you go?" Also, ask something like, "Where do you stand on the whole God thing?," or "Do you ever think about Christianity?" Write a symbol on your hand in permanent ink to remind yourself to ask someone one of these questions before the ink washes off. Once you do, you will have opened the door to begin evangelizing someone! *Read today's Scripture.*

Now, in this chapter of Acts, God breaks down Peter's prejudice against Gentiles (non-Jews), and we see another outpouring of the Holy Spirit just like the one in Acts 2, only this one was over Gentiles. Cornelius's prayer life and acts of charity were an offering to God (verse 4). Let that be said of your prayer life, my student! Too often, our prayers are exclusively requests of God, but Cornelius's prayers along with his giving to the poor rose up to God like an offering. That's awesome!

What can be your symbol to remind you to share your faith?

Dwell

PHILIPPIANS 4:4–9

Have you asked someone one of those questions from yesterday's devotional yet? If not, get on it! If you have, then pray right now that the Holy Spirit would work on that person's heart. Pray God's protection over him. Ask the Father to draw him in (John 6:44). *Read today's Scripture.*

When we were drowning in grief, there was this creeping notion we might go through life forever broken, ever trudging through the pieces of what was once a happy life but could never truly be again as our family would never again be complete on this earth. God has given us a peace that cannot be understood and it guards our hearts (verse 7). It's beautiful. Paul tells us twice in the same verse to rejoice! Because the Lord is near (verse 5), we shouldn't worry about anything (verse 6)! It's on this foundation that He lays out this awesome set of standards for us to focus on and "dwell" on. That word *dwell*: do you know what it means? It means to think about something deeply. All of these teachings collide to form a basis for unshakable joy.

What does *dwell* mean to you and your faith?

Proof God Exists

MATTHEW 16:21–23

If you find yourself having to argue to prove that God exists, don't worry. You will learn as you grow as a Christian and you've got the Holy Spirit as your ally! *Read today's Scripture.*

This is a pretty bone-headed moment for Peter. Jesus had told His disciples many times He would be killed and would then rise again. Peter hasn't been listening and is so overwhelmed by the thought of Jesus' death that he refuses to believe it. In saying, "This will never happen to You" (verse 22), Peter is denying that Jesus will do the very thing He was born to do, so Jesus rebukes him. Pray now that you would have only the things of God on your mind today and the things that concern us as mortal men would just fade to the background.

Write out a prayer that asks for help as you keep your life focused on God.

_____

_____

_____

_____

_____

_____

_____

_____

_____

_____

_____

_____

_____

_____

Called Out

ACTS 11:1–26

In today's Scripture, Peter is getting called out by his fellow Jews for evangelizing Gentiles. It's fascinating because Jesus faced similar criticism for ministering to tax collectors, sinners, and even a woman with an adulterous reputation. I hope you're the kind of man who will associate with and minister to absolutely anyone no matter what is said about you. Watch as Peter silences his critics in verses 1–18 and then get ready to have your mind blown by what God does through Stephen's execution in verses 19–26. When you get to verse 20, that word *Hellenists* refers to Greek people who worshipped false gods. *Read today's Scripture.*

What looked like a victory for Satan became the driving force behind the gospel's move outward from Jerusalem just as Jesus prophesied would happen in Acts 1:8! Talk about God working through all things (Romans 8:28)! They thought they killed the movement when they killed Stephen, but they just ended up inventing the term *Christians* that we use today (verse 26). So, I want you to *go all Acts 11 on this day.* Evangelize someone *today.* After Day 75, we are going to coach this person to evangelize someone else.

Who can you share the gospel with today?

_____

_____

_____

_____

_____

_____

_____

_____

_____

_____

_____

_____

_____

_____

Joy

PHILIPPIANS 4:10–14

The things in my life that bring me the greatest joy are things that have nothing to do with my bank account. My bride's beautiful smile costs no money at all. My sons' voices coming from the backseat of my truck are completely unaffected by money. Making music next to a fire pit surrounded by family and friends is free. The ocean does not charge me for use of its waves. The fact that I'm saved will never be revoked even if all of my possessions are taken away. That I am heaven-bound can never be robbed of me. I can do anything through God who gives me strength. I can face lean times and still keep my joy because my joy isn't rooted in worldly things. *Read today's Scripture.*

I pray your life overflows with joy. I pray your joy is bigger than circumstances. Your joy is precious to God, despised by Satan, and worth fighting for. Let your joy be rooted in your salvation. Let your joy overflow. Let your joy be contagious and start an epidemic today!

How can you share your joy?

_____

_____

_____

_____

_____

_____

_____

_____

_____

_____

_____

_____

_____

_____

You Gotta Pay

MATTHEW 17:24–27

Being a Christian will cost you everything, but you'll encounter some Christians who aren't willing to pay anything. They may have been led to Christ without understanding the nature of sin and repentance from it. They're taken off guard by what they find in church membership and living the Christian life. They're like the person Jesus describes in Luke 14:28 who set out to build a tower without first counting its cost. Such is the Christian who isn't willing to give anything. You gotta pay. *Read today's Scripture.*

This is a seldom-taught miracle and its context reveals something amazing. These guys changed the whole world by the power of the Holy Spirit! When you envision the events of the book of Acts, don't imagine old dudes with gray hair doing these amazing things by the power of God. Instead correctly envision young men performing these miracles and be inspired to be used of God in a similar way.

Make a list of how you can be used by God.

_____

_____

_____

_____

_____

_____

_____

_____

_____

_____

_____

_____

_____

_____

_____

God-Sized Prayers

ACTS 12:5–19

Write on your Acts Axe bookmark a prayer to God asking Him to do something mighty through you today and leave room on it for your follow-up story at the end of the day. When the people of God pray earnestly in accordance with the will of God, walls come down. So pray, Christian, and as you pray, be inspired by this prayer in verse 5 that is answered in verses 6–14 which leaves the believers in verses 15–19 speechless. *Read today's Scripture.*

I find it genuinely funny that Peter, having seen some powerful stuff already, thought that he was experiencing a vision (verse 9). He was shackled between two dudes because King Herod was paranoid and put a total of eighteen soldiers in charge of guarding him. Can you imagine being one of those guys? I wonder if the older soldiers make the rookies do it. Ha! Now, look at how the answer to Mary, Rhoda, and the other believers' prayers is literally knocking at their door in verse 13. Now that you're a Christian, it's time to pray big God-sized prayers that align with God's will.

Write down what you asked God to do through you today!

_____

_____

_____

_____

_____

_____

_____

_____

_____

_____

_____

_____

_____

_____

_____

Apocalyptic Prophecy

2 THESSALONIANS 2:1–17

Go take a look back at your Acts Axe bookmark and write in the story of what God did when you asked Him to use you mightily yesterday. Cool, huh? Now, we're going to look at an apocalyptic prophecy. Now that you're a Christian, belief in what the Bible says about the world's tomorrows has an impact on your today. The book of Revelation is not the only book of the Bible that describes God's plan for the world. The book of Daniel, some of Jesus' teachings (see Matthew 24), John's writings, and this letter that the Holy Spirit inspired Paul to write to the church of Thessalonica teach us more. Remembering that the Day of the Lord is the Second Coming of Jesus and that the "man of lawlessness" is the antichrist (the beast in the book of Revelation). *Read today's Scripture.*

Not all miracles are performed for good. The antichrist will be surrounded by miracles that deceive unrighteous people into worshipping him. However, as we live our lives in expectation for what God has planned, we live our lives for the One who will be victorious over this evil with just a breath (verse 8)!

What did God do in your life?

_____

_____

_____

_____

_____

_____

_____

_____

_____

_____

_____

_____

_____

_____

Conflict

MATTHEW 18:15–20

I just spoke with a former student of mine about this. A guy in the church he joined for his time away at college sinned in a way that devastated another church member. He was confronted one-on-one, then by a group, and the pastor and some leaders are speaking with him tonight. It's rare for things to reach this point in the process called "church discipline." I've only seen it come to step three twice before. I'll tell you how it turned out after you *read today's Scripture.*

This is the definitive go-to passage for dealing with conflict in the church. If someone sins against you, then . . . brace yourself to have your mind blown . . . seriously, hold onto something right now because too many Christians apparently don't get this earth-shattering truth . . . you talk to him about it. What? Whoa! Yes, and you forgive him. Keep reading Matthew 18 through to verse 35 see how to forgive (from the heart) and how many times you should forgive him (ten times what you think). I have seen this literally God-given model bring rebellious Christians to repentance. It truly does restore people. We'll look more at handling conflict with other Christians in our upcoming study of 1 John.

What ideas do you have to handle conflict with friends, siblings, and parents?

The Plans I Have for You

ACTS 13:1–12

In my Student Ministry, we have this catch phrase to summarize the most common prayer request among my oldest students. When someone says, "I'll have the classic," he's saying, "Pray for me that I could figure out the specifics of God's will for me." One of the fascinating things I see as a pastor who has worked with thousands of students is young people growing into their future as Christians and no two students are identical. God has fashioned you for a specific purpose. *Read today's Scripture.*

Now, I know that, given the whole "God's apostle showing up and blinding (in a similar way to his own experience) this sorcerer" thing, my choice of focus for this text might seem odd, but hear me on this . . . and by "hear" I mean "read." Simeon, Lucius, and Manaen were *incredible* men of God with *incredible* talents, stories, and connections. For crying out loud, Manaen was a close friend of King Herod's! Yet, God chose Paul and Barnabas for this purpose to the exclusion of the others: they were meant for something else. Just as the men in this text did, worship and fast today that you might hear the Holy Spirit's plans for you.

What plans for you have you heard from the Holy Spirit?

_____

_____

_____

_____

_____

_____

_____

_____

_____

_____

_____

_____

_____

_____

_____

Is God Calling?

1 TIMOTHY 4:7–16

The book of 1 Timothy is one of Paul's letters to a young guy who was the pastor of a humongous church. Chapters 2 and 3 are instructions on how to structure a church's leadership with qualified deacons and elders as well as worship instructions. Chapter 5 is about paying your pastor well, and chapter 6 is about false teachers. Now, however, we're just going to get an introduction by looking at chapter 4. *Read today's Scripture.*

The sword I told you about earlier that hangs in my office was given to me at my ordination where a counsel of pastors and deacons prayed over me in a ceremony that was based on verse 14. Being a young guy in ministry, verse 12 is a big deal to me and it should be to you, too. God could be calling you into the ministry full-time as a pastor, worship pastor, or missionary, but because of the Great Commission (Matthew 28:18–20), we're *all* called to do ministry in some way or another. Begin yours as a young man by living according to verse 12 and prayerfully consider now the idea that you might have a job in ministry one day!

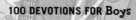

Can you imagine a job in full-time ministry?

Servant Leadership

MATTHEW 20:20–28

Jesus gives us the ultimate example of "servant leadership." Even if you aren't a leader in any official capacity, the act of living the Christian life in front of your peers is a form of leadership because it *influences* others. What Jesus teaches about the nature of leadership in a perfect sense overturned the teachings of His day. *Read today's Scripture.*

Check your heart against this passage now. Be real with yourself. Ask, "Am I promoting myself to make myself a bigger deal, or am I trying to make Christ a bigger deal?" Jesus had every single right to show up in kingly splendor, kick the door down to any palace, and shout self-indulgent orders at the servants, but He didn't. Instead, He did things like wash His betrayer's feet and tell us to do the same. Jesus had perfect integrity. He not only spoke this teaching to us, He also modeled this teaching for us. Just as John the Baptist said in John 3:30, Jesus must become greater and you and I must become less. Now, let that be your motto for today. Tonight, write on your Matt Marker about how this approach made today different from yesterday.

How can you be a servant leader?

_____

_____

_____

_____

_____

_____

_____

_____

_____

_____

_____

_____

_____

_____

_____

Unpopular Truths

ACTS 13:42–52

There is a real hatred out there for Christians. Online especially, there are many people who just want to "troll" Christians to get a rouse out of them and any discussion that takes place is likely going to be fruitless. Now, sometimes those discussions can be very impactful and you need to be sensitive to the Holy Spirit's confirmation and take words given to you by the Holy Spirit in those moments (Mark 13:11), but in today's Scripture, the disciples are actually happy to be moving on from a town full of spiteful people. *Check out today's Scripture.*

Paul and Barnabas are boldly speaking the truth about how God once sovereignly chose the nation of Israel and the people who joined them in Old Testament worship, but today's salvation is for Gentiles too (verse 46). This is a really unpopular thing to have said to this crowd, but they said it anyway. Do you have the guts to speak the unpopular truths of God? Part of what made them so happy to be leaving is not only the evangelistic fruit that it bore (verse 48), but also the fact that their consciences were clear because they had spoken the truth.

Where is it hardest for you to share your faith?

_____

_____

_____

_____

_____

_____

_____

_____

_____

_____

_____

_____

_____

_____

Serve

TITUS 1:1–9

According to Ephesians 4 and this passage in Titus, the pastor's job is to equip *you* for the work of ministry. If all the members of a church expect the pastor to be at their disposal at all times, that church will not grow past a certain point because that pastor only has so many minutes in a day. However, if the people of a church see it as their job to do the work of ministry under the guidance of their pastor, then the church has no ceiling! *Read today's Scripture.*

Paul discipled Titus and did ministry alongside the way Moses did with Joshua. Moses' father-in-law Jethro (what a rugged lumberjack name) saw Moses hearing every single issue from every single Israelite. Jethro called him out on it and gave him a brilliant system (Exodus 18:13–27) that allowed other people to do the work of ministry so that more ministry could be done. In the New Testament, we see this played out through the roles of deacons and elders beginning in Acts 6:1–7 and expounded upon in today's Scripture. Be a colaborer with your pastor. Now that you're a Christian, it's time to serve in your church!

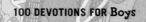

How and where can you serve?

_____

_____

_____

_____

_____

_____

_____

_____

_____

_____

_____

_____

_____

_____

Prayer Life

MATTHEW 21:12–13

My student, I hope your prayer life is an intimate two-way experience of communication with God. I hope you pray often and not just for yourself, but for your church as well. In fact, we're going to practice the discipline of praying for your church today. Look at Jesus' fiercely protective heart for His church in *today's Scripture*.

I love my church. We've had fun in my church family doing ministry together and having these cool experiences. Now, give yourself some sort of a reminder now to pray for your church all day today. As you can see with the table flipping, Jesus was fed up with people being ripped off and shouts Isaiah 56:7 at them; reminding them that the church is to be a house of prayer. So, make a note on your Leaping Leaflet to pray for your church all day today!

What is your prayer for your church? Write it down.

_____

_____

_____

_____

_____

_____

_____

_____

_____

_____

_____

_____

_____

_____

Keep Evangelizing

ACTS 14:1–7

If you didn't follow through with it yesterday, give yourself a reminder maybe on your phone's calendar app, or just an old-school string tied around your finger to spend the day today praying that God would bless your church and grow it as more and more people are saved! *Read today's Scripture.*

On your Acts Axe, draw a tiny picture of yourself on the far left side, a big thick wall with room to write inside on the middle, and the person whom you're being called to evangelize on the other side of the wall from you. On the wall, write all the things that would keep you from reaching out to that person today. Now, compare all the things on that wall to the insane persecution that the apostles faced in today's Scripture. I seriously doubt that you're worried about your government officials led by an angry and diverse mob plotting to pummel you with rocks until you die. That's what the apostles faced in today's Scripture, but verse 7 says they kept evangelizing! So, what excuse do we have? Would those excuses fly with someone like Paul? What would Paul's wall drawing contain?

What excuses do we use not to evangelize?

_____

_____

_____

_____

_____

_____

_____

_____

_____

_____

_____

_____

_____

Snotless

HEBREWS 12:1–3

Reader, meet the book of Hebrews. The previous chapter is called the "Hall of Faith" and the idea is that you would read Hebrews 11 and hope to join its ranks, to wonder what it would say about you if there were a forty-first verse that read, "By faith [your name here] performed [act of faith "x"]." From there, the first words of today's Scripture take that idea and build on it to give us this practical challenge. *Read today's Scripture.*

The words "since we also have such a large cloud of witnesses surrounding us" paint a picture of these great men and women of faith named in Hebrews 11 watching us! It's a cool thought and it motivates the snot out of me. Seriously, I have no snot right now. I am snotless. The idea of seeing someone like Paul in heaven and hearing him say, "You did some pretty decent work down there, Campbell" fires me up! So, just as today's text says, throw aside everything in your life that is slowing you down and finish the race well. There's a righteous (literally righteous) party at the finish line!

What in your life is slowing you down?

God Hates Figs?

MATTHEW 21:18–22

This is one of those really obscure, but deeply fascinating miracles of Jesus' ministry. It will make more sense the first time you read it if you know ahead of time that the fig tree represents Israel, that Jesus just drove the money changers out of the temple right before this, and that we can learn lessons from the Old Testament by remembering that God dealt with Old Testament Israel in a similar way to how He deals with us. *Read today's Scripture.*

So, what can we learn from this? Is it that God hates figs? Yes, my student. Yes, it is. Nah, I'm kidding. Israel, based on the terrible spiritual shape the temple was just in when Jesus left it, was not bearing fruit. Make it your heart's earnest prayer that God would not come to find you bearing no fruit. Write this prayer out on your Matt Marker now. My prayer for my students is the same as my prayer for you and it is taken directly from Philippians 1:9–11, that you would be filled with the fruit of righteousness!

What do you think it means to be filled with the fruit of righteousness?

_____

_____

_____

_____

_____

_____

_____

_____

_____

_____

_____

_____

_____

Spiritual Warfare

ACTS 14:21–28

Now that you're a Christian, you're going to face suffering that you would not have faced if you were still lost. I know that's not happy blue raspberry flavored good news, but it's true. Having aligned yourself with God, you align yourself against Satan and now find yourself in the middle of a spiritual war. These trials and difficulties are necessary, God is still good regardless of them, God has a purpose for them, and He will bring you to the other side a stronger Christian. *Read today's Scripture.*

Take heart, my student. Don't let your heart be troubled. See your difficulties as necessary (verse 22) and see them as new chapters in your testimony. Share openly and honestly about the difficulties you have in your life so you would see them bear fruit for the kingdom of God (verse 27). Then, you will know with beautiful results the answer to that classic question (called the question of "Theodicy") why God allows bad things to happen to people.

What difficulties do you see in your life?

Verdicts

JAMES 1:2–4

If you aren't right in the middle of a time of difficulty and trial right now, it's only a matter of time. Trials are an integral part of being a Christian and, like any trial, these trials have verdicts. Let the verdict of every one of your trials be that you refused to forsake God even when it may have looked like He had forsaken you. *Read today's Scripture.*

This passage doesn't call us to pretend like we're happy about our trials. It tells us to be happy that we're going to develop perseverance and made more mature; not lacking anything as a result of our passing this faith test. Peak ahead also to verse 12 for an amazing word of encouragement in the midst of trial. Now, write on your Leaping Leaflet the words, "I've already made my mind up that my faith is going to pass this test even if I stumble on the way. I've already made my mind up that I'm going to continue to praise God through this trial!" Write these words and mean them with every ounce of your masculine soul.

Finish this sentence. "I've made my mind up to..."

_____

_____

_____

_____

_____

_____

_____

_____

_____

_____

_____

_____

_____

_____

Righteous War Path

MATTHEW 21:23–27 AND 1 PETER 3:15

Did you write that commitment of faith on your Leaping Leaflet yesterday? If not, write it now on your forehead in permanent marker. No, I'm just kidding, don't do that. Instead, *read today's Scripture.*

All throughout Matthew 21, Jesus is on this righteous war path. Some stories from the Gospels show Jesus slipping and disappearing into the crowd because it wasn't yet time for Him to really put up a fight, but the gloves are off throughout all of Matthew 21. Here, Jesus refuses to let His opponents set the rules for the debate. When an atheist asks you a question, remember he lacks the authority to set the debate's terms. He doesn't even have an explanation for how physical matter came into existence out of nothing-ness. Refuse to accept the foundation on which your opponent's question is built if he is coming at you in hostility with a trap set for you.

How can you always stand your ground in your faith?

Imperfections

ACTS 15:36–41

Now that you're a Christian, you'll see more and more of the imperfections of the church as a whole. Denominations are an okay thing; they really are. Some modern denominations are offshoots from churches begun by some of the most theologically gifted minds of the reformation (a time when protestant denominations split from the Catholic Church). However, some denominations were born out of conflict, sin, terrible errors in Bible interpretation, and even the deception of the enemy. Conflict with other believers is going to happen; even between anointed men of God. *Read today's Scripture.*

Whoa, so Barnabas was stuck between Paul and John Mark. Paul didn't trust John Mark not to desert them again! Yet, God used even these conflicts to bring about something beautiful. Instead of one church planting team, there were two! Because of this conflict, their reach was doubled. Give God your conflicts and ask Him to use them in the growth of His kingdom. Then, your conflicts serve a beautiful purpose even if they were born from ugly things.

What conflicts can you turn over to God?

Doubleheader

JAMES 1:5–21

You seriously have to read this whole chapter when you get the chance because it is a rapid-fire series of life-changing truths all back-to-back. The first chapter of James alone teaches about trials, riches, temptation, gifts from God, anger, keeping our mouths shut, holiness, how to read the Bible, to looking after orphans and widows. *Read today's Scripture.*

Get ready for a double header. We have two challenges from this text. Based on verses 5–8, you're going to fully believe God will answer your prayers when you pray to Him for wisdom. Second, you're going to take an old-school monk-style vow of silence for a given amount of time! This is so cool to me. Go for at least six waking hours and finish out with a legit understanding of verses 5–8. Now, *ssshhhhh!*

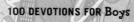

What did you learn in your time of silence?

Shocking Truth

MATTHEW 21:33–46

This chapter of Matthew is the focus of a message video series I taught from the peak of one of the highest mountains in North Carolina. To help you understand it, remember the vineyard owner is God, the tenant farmers are the Pharisees, the slaves are the prophets of the Old Testament (who were killed), and the son is Jesus. *Read today's Scripture.*

The shocking truth of verse 42 is that the kingdom of God, which had (and still has as of the year 2014) belonged to the Jews for so long, was about to belong to more than Jews: it was about to belong to all who would believe (Joel 2:32; Acts 2:21; Romans 10:13). This was a blow to the gut for first-century Jews. Now, what I see Jesus doing in this chapter is cutting out the feel-good stuff and speaking only the hard-core truths. Christians are not supposed to be marshmallows all the time. Go Matthew 21 on this world every now and then.

What does Matthew 21 mean to you?

_____

_____

_____

_____

_____

_____

_____

_____

_____

_____

_____

_____

_____

_____

Fruit

ACTS 16:11–15, 40

Share the gospel with someone with the hopes of that person coming to faith in Christ *today*. If you've already done that through the course of this book, then speak with that person *today* about leading yet *another* person to Christ. This is to say that I want the person whom you have led to Christ to lead another person to Christ. I want the fruit of your spiritual life to bear spiritual fruit itself. This was the essence of the Great Commission! *Read today's Scripture.*

So, Lydia, who was saved at the beginning of the chapter, ministered to those saved at the chapter's end. The first time I flew away from Brazil, I thought, *There's no way all of those people whom I led to Christ were really getting what I was saying to them.* The next year, as my bus approached the small "hotel," hundreds of people burst out of their tents and ran alongside the bus. These were the people we had led to Christ the year before. When I couldn't find a translator, I had to depend upon Lucas and Thiago who lead this one "troublemaker" to Christ. I stood there and wept. It was amazing!

Who do you plan to share the gospel with?

_____

_____

_____

_____

_____

_____

_____

_____

_____

_____

_____

_____

_____

_____

Results

JAMES 1:22–27

Read today's Scripture. If you're a Christian, then your faith in Christ is going to actually produce results. Your study of the Bible will not result in some trivial knowledge of the Bible, but will result in you actually *doing what the Bible says to do.* According to today's text (along with Matthew 7), unless you actually *do* the will of God and do not merely *know* the will of God, you're likely not saved, and your faith is dead and therefore useless (James 1:26).

Now, you can't earn your salvation by doing something in accordance with the will of God. Instead, the fact that you're already living in accordance with God's will would prove that you are saved. So, today, not because it saves you but because you are already saved, evangelize. Evangelize because God's Word tells us to. Do not merely read the Great Commission in Matthew 28:18–20 (our first devotional together in this book) and so deceive yourself, do what it says and do it today. In doing what God's Word says, you will be blessed (James 1:25)!

What action have you taken to do what God's Word says?

_____

_____

_____

_____

_____

_____

_____

_____

_____

_____

_____

_____

_____

Taxes

MATTHEW 22:15–22

We are blessed to be able to give. It is an honor and a sweet act of worship to tithe, and my wife and I love it. When we have some unexpected income, we genuinely get excited that we now have even more to give to God and His church. It's the same thing as singing a worship song. We also love to give offerings; lifting people up who need help. Paying taxes, however . . . I would rather feed my toes one-at-a-time to caffeinated piranhas . . . but I've still got to do it. *Read today's Scripture.*

So, tithe, Christian. More than that, give offerings to special causes and individual cases. When you get an allowance, divide the amount by ten and give that tenth to the church. For example, if you get paid $100 for something, you would give the church $10 from it. Now, there's also this putrid thing called "taxes." Ugh. When I give my son Austin (whom we call "Cozy") a snack, I take a big bite first and call it the "Daddy tax." Give to your governing authorities, or "Caesar," what they charge you and give back to God a portion of that which He's given you.

What will you give to your church this week?

_____

_____

_____

_____

_____

_____

_____

_____

_____

_____

_____

_____

_____

_____

Evangelism

ACTS 17:22–34

Look at how gifted Paul is in evangelism. Yes, we are all called to evangelize, but there is a spiritual gift in evangelism (Ephesians 4:11) and Paul definitely had it. Spiritual gifts are abilities and callings that the Holy Spirit gives to each Christian. God tends to call people of varying gifts to the same church so that, even at a smaller church, you have every gift represented by at least one person. This makes the church like a human body in which each part serves a purpose that is different from the others and all of those parts combined achieve something that one of them could not by itself. In this text, Paul is using his gift to evangelize. *Read today's Scripture.*

It's amazing. Paul just used a pagan altar as a transition to the gospel of Jesus Christ! He met people where they were and spoke in terms they could understand. The Holy Spirit drew and some people were saved (verse 34)! So, keep this in mind as you evangelize today and let it inspire you. Speak to people in terms they can understand and watch the Holy Spirit work. Remember, we're going to encourage the one you evangelize to evangelize someone else!

Make a new list of people to talk to about Jesus.

Trials

1 PETER 1:3–9

Now that you're a Christian, you need to understand what your spiritual gifts are and put them to use in your church. This is a huge deal! Your spiritual gifts are a massive piece to the puzzle of God's specific will for you. *Read today's Scripture.*

The loss of my son Aiden has left me with more confidence in my faith than ever. Now that I've stood at my son's grave and praised God, I know for a fact I can praise God anywhere after anything. The trials in your life serve a purpose. They prove your faith to be genuine. As we saw in James 2, trials in your life are to be seen as opportunities. You are to face them with a sense of vision. See in your mind what will be. Know that God is going to use your trials to shape you into a stronger Christian. Sometimes, God allows them so precisely that we'll return to Him in our hearts.

What trial have you gone through that has strengthened your faith?

_____

_____

_____

_____

_____

_____

_____

_____

_____

_____

_____

_____

_____

_____

_____

_____

_____

His Own Authority

MATTHEW 22:23–33

Before Jesus' teaching ministry began (probably when He was thirty years old in His physical form), Jewish teachers called "rabbis" would teach by building on the authority of other rabbis. They would do what you'll have to do in this tedious, but so incredibly good for you, school assignment called a "research paper" and, that is, cite their sources. To cite (pronounced just like "sight") your source is to share with your listener or reader the writings or speeches from which you learned your information. Jesus, however, taught in this ground-breaking new way. He didn't cite any source. He was *His own* authority and no one had ever taught this way. *Read today's Scripture.*

By now, you've seen this astonishing effect Jesus has on crowds. I preach for large crowds and, as one who teaches the words of Jesus straight from the Bible, I can tell you He still has this effect. Here, He teaches about marriage and heaven, but He mostly calls out the Sadducees. The Sadducees were sad, you see. Ha! If you disbelieve in the resurrection like the Sadducees (verse 23), then you disbelieve in the power of God (verse 29) and cannot be saved (1 Corinthians 15:12–20).

What kinds of things could be "called out" in your life?

_____

_____

_____

_____

_____

_____

_____

_____

_____

_____

_____

_____

_____

_____

Jesus Is the Truth

ACTS 18:24–28

The verses in the "EvangeRap" teach the lost person about God's love (John 3:16), about our sin (Romans 3:23), about how our sin separates us from God (Romans 6:23), about how Jesus is the truth and we must answer to Him (John 14:6), and about how we are saved if we confess that Jesus is Lord and believe wholeheartedly in His resurrection (Romans 10:9). You're going to teach it to your friend you led to the Lord recently. If you haven't evangelized yet, review the EvangeRap and give someone a chance to respond to the gospel *today. Read today's Scripture.*

So, this couple Priscilla and Aquila saw the potential in this young whippersnapper Apollos (verse 24), set him straight theologically (verse 26), and then unleashed him to do ministry (verses 27 and 28). That's similar to what you're going to do. Today, see the potential in your newly evangelized friend. See his potential as a force for the kingdom of God, plug him into your church, introduce him to your pastor, teach him the EvangeRap, and then set him loose on the lost.

How can you help build the faith of friends who are new Christians?

_____

_____

_____

_____

_____

_____

_____

_____

_____

_____

_____

_____

_____

Danger!

1 PETER 1:10–16

The book of 1 Peter is dangerous. Christians were outlaws when it was written and these outlaw Christians were tougher than nails. They often faced horrid persecution. They met secretly in underground rooms built for graves. They communicated in code out in public (this is where our "Jesus" fish was born), and if someone didn't show up to church, it may have meant that he was arrested, or possibly even executed. With that original context in mind, *read today's Scripture.*

First Peter's calls to put our hope in heaven (verse 13) and its teachings on joy in the midst of trial (1:6–9) are even more powerful when read in light of their original context. These people praised God and led holy lives as they were facing slaughter. In the face of your trials, in your darkest hour of night, praise God, Christian. Be holy, Christian. Through your trial, you keep your focus on heaven where we'll be for *eternity.* Your trial's going to end, but even if it lasted one hundred years, that century of torture doesn't compare to your coming eternity of paradise (2 Corinthians 4:17).

How can you keep your focus on heaven?

Love, Christian

MATTHEW 22:34–40

In *What It Means to Be a Christian*, we studied several examples of Old Testament prophecies regarding the Messiah that were fulfilled in the New Testament. Pointing out the fact that these books were written over a millennium apart from one another, sharing these scriptural truths can be a profoundly convincing apologetic (meaning it can convince people of the truth of Christianity) as we saw in Apollos's ministry on Day 81. We also studied today's Scripture, but my heart leaps at the thought that you may have been saved *as you read* my previous book and now are returning to this same passage as a Christian. *Read today's Scripture.*

Love, Christian. This love for God will result in a love for people. The Old Testament's commands to eat, worship, and conduct a society in a certain way are fulfilled (Matthew 5:17) and the new commands we're given in the New Testament including the Great Commission all come down to just *loving* (John 13:34–35). In fact, the Old Testament prophets and the Old Testament laws were all leading to this call to love as well (verse 40). Write on your Matt Marker that you're committed to Matthew 22's Great Commandments!

Write down your commitment to Matthew 22.

_____

_____

_____

_____

_____

_____

_____

_____

_____

_____

_____

_____

_____

_____

His Holy Spirit

ACTS 19:1–7

As my family sits down to eat dinner (which is often something Cajun, Italian, or Mexican), I pray over not only our food, but over my family as well. Recently, I prayed that God would fill my family with His Holy Spirit and the results have been utterly amazing. It's true that, if we just ask God for more of the Holy Spirit in our lives, He will give it to us because He is a good Father (Luke 11:13). See also Acts 5:32, Romans 5:5, and 1 Thessalonians 4:8. *Read today's Scripture.*

Have you ever been to a church like this one Paul stumbles upon? They didn't even know there was a Holy Spirit! Some Christians are like this today. They worship the Father and know about the Son, but don't know a thing about the Holy Spirit. On your Acts Axe, write out a prayer asking God to fill you with the Holy Spirit today, that you would go about your day and see the Holy Spirit move in amazing ways as it overflows from your heart to touch the hearts of others.

Write out your prayer, and ask the Holy Spirit
to move in your heart.

Love Purely

1 PETER 1:22–25

Read today's Scripture. These persecuted Christians who were scattered around the Roman Empire were sent a divinely inspired letter from Peter. There are so many different things such a letter could say, but this letter says the perfect thing because its Inspirer is perfect. It could have given them military strategy. It could have taught them to perform physical miracles. It could have contained anything, but it contained a command to love one another and to stand by the Word of God. That's what these Christians who were being persecuted by the crazed emperor Nero were taught, and it applies to us today in the midst of our trials.

You stand by your Bible. Believe the whole thing and never back down. Love fiercely. Be ever forgiving of your fellow Christians as they forgive you (Ephesians 4:2). When you love, love with a pure and honest heart (verse 22). When, in the face of trial, you choose to love others by standing upon the Bible, you set an example to other believers (1 Thessalonians 1:5–7). So, what will happen to our heroes in the persecuted church of Rome in the year 64? Tune in next time!

How can you learn to love purely?

Pride

MATTHEW 23:1–12

It's a dangerous thing when a Christian gets prideful about how humble he is. Think about that for a minute. Then, *read today's Scripture.*

Beware of pride, my student. It is toxic to your soul, but its symptoms are invisible to the one infected by it. It took me *years* to realize that I was a prideaholic. Even though my dad and brother spoke to me directly about it, I didn't listen. It took God humbling me for me to finally get it. Please, don't be like me and learn this Matthew 23 Pharisee lesson the hard way. When we exalt ourselves, God humbles us and that's serious business. It can be insanely painful. Instead, humble yourself before God without the expectation that you'll ever be exalted. That's what humility truly is and, quite beautifully, these are the kinds of people God chooses to have exalted (1 Peter 5:6; Proverbs 27:2). Go right now to the mirror and, as you look *honestly* at yourself, ask God to reveal to you any lingering sin of pride that may be in your heart. Take practical steps today to live out humility. Do this, content to never be praised for it.

What is God revealing to you?

_____

_____

_____

_____

_____

_____

_____

_____

_____

_____

_____

_____

_____

_____

Mimic Me Please

ACTS 20:7–12

I was serious about looking in the mirror and praying yesterday. If you haven't done it yet, do it now. If you did it, you may want to do it again. Then, get ready to have your mind blown by this scary/awesome story in *today's Scripture.*

So, what did we learn? *If you fall asleep in church . . . you die.* Ha! Nah, I'm just kidding . . . sort of. Paul's giving his farewell message to the church of Troas before he goes on what will likely be a deadly mission trip to Jerusalem. As Paul speaks on and on, young Eutychus (pronounced "you-ti-cuss") gets overwhelmed by the oil lamp smoke that's flowing out through the window he's sitting in (verses 8–9). What's particularly powerful to me is how what Paul does both has roots in the Old Testament prophets Elijah and Elisha (2 Kings 4:32–37 and 1 Kings 17:19–24) and how it so closely resembles evangelism. When you obey the Great Commission and share the gospel with someone who becomes saved, you are seeing the dead come to life. That is evangelism! Just as Elisha mimicked Elijah, may your newly evangelized friend mimic you by evangelizing.

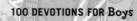

Who might be mimicking you?

_____

_____

_____

_____

_____

_____

_____

_____

_____

_____

_____

_____

_____

_____

_____

_____

Facing Trials

1 PETER 3:13–18

Read today's Scripture. As you can see, facing trials is (or at least is *going to be*) a big part of your Christianity. When (notice I didn't write "if") trials come your way, remember the original recipients of 1 Peter. They won! Though many Christians were slaughtered, the church survived and eventually grew to comprise a political majority that influenced even the emperor by the year 300! Now, this sort of persecution and the emboldening effect it has on Christians is still happening today. Ask your pastor about the church in China and North Korea. God uses persecution and trial to bear fruit.

I've mentioned my son Aiden before. When he died I preached a message at his funeral. That message led to the salvation of several new Christians both when it was first broadcast and at every event I've taught at around the world. Hundreds of people have been saved through that testimony. Now, ask me why my son died. Ask me why my family faces this trial. I'll tell you it is so that people would be reconciled to God. I'll tell you it happened to bear fruit for God's kingdom.

Are there hard things in your life that God can use?

_____

_____

_____

_____

_____

_____

_____

_____

_____

_____

_____

_____

_____

_____

Selfies

MATTHEW 23:25–28

You know what cultural phenomenon I think is both funny and lame? Selfies! With that in mind, here's another passage that we covered in *What It Means to Be a Christian* that may mean something new to you if you're reading it for the first time as a Christian. *Read today's Scripture.*

In our "selfie" culture, people want to put out only the best possible representation of themselves and not the most honest representation. This same behavior goes on in church when someone shows up ready to outwardly put on some fantastic show but is actually rotting away inside (verse 27). In reality, this well-painted Christian is drowning in secret sin, or isn't actually saved. Be the young man who helps your pastor bring about a culture of authenticity (being real) in your church. Put away the selfies and speak the truth (Ephesians 4:25). If it doesn't exist in your church already, ask your pastor to establish for you a group of guys who confess sin to one another, pray for one another, and experience authentic spiritual healing with one another (James 5:16).

Are you in a group? Write down the names of those in your group, and pray for them.

_____

_____

_____

_____

_____

_____

_____

_____

_____

_____

_____

_____

_____

Your Story

ACTS 22:1–22

I've shared some of my testimony with you about how God has brought about such beautiful things through my son Aiden. What's so cool about that to me is that it makes you a part of my testimony. I was saved when I was a small boy, but as a grown man, my testimony is that God has been faithful to me all along, especially through the greatest pain a father could know. Today, Paul stands before the critics and shares his testimony . . . and it ends with them wanting to kill him for it. Ha! *Read today's Scripture.*

So, this is a big part of how you both evangelize and encourage others to evangelize: you tell your story. You share your testimony. If you've never shared your testimony before, you can iron out the wrinkles and build up your confidence by going to a private place and rehearsing it. Some people may not be open right away to hearing the Scriptures of the EvangeRap, but they will at least hear you out when you tell them your story. What are they going to do? Correct you? *You're* the world's leading expert on *your* testimony. So, share it with confidence today.

Begin to write down your story.

_____

_____

_____

_____

_____

_____

_____

_____

_____

_____

_____

_____

_____

Gnosticism

1 JOHN 1:5–10

Books of the Bible are best understood, appreciated, and interpreted if we know what God was doing in the lives of those who wrote it and the lives of those who first received it. There was once an uprising. The church was infiltrated by an ancient religion known as "Gnosticism," which is pronounced "nosti-sizm." Followers of Gnosticism are Gnostics and the Gnostics who tried to sabotage the newborn Christian church with their infiltration and their fake "gospel" writings (found in the Nag Hamadi scrolls) get a whooping in the book of 1 John. *Read today's Scripture.*

Speaking of conflict, *recently* I went head-to-head with pastors who don't take the Bible literally like I do. (To take the Bible literally means you believe the *whole* Bible.) Our Bible, as evangelical Protestants, was formed through a series of events including meticulous and protective monks, scrutinous and honest historians, and a series of huge meetings (like the Council of Nicea) involving hundreds of great men of God. False, unreliable, or unnecessary teachings (like those of the Apocrypha in the Roman Catholic and Eastern Orthodox Bibles or the Nag Hamadi scrolls) were not allowed into the canon of Scripture we call our Bible.

How many of the books of the Bible can you list in order? Go.

_____

_____

_____

_____

_____

_____

_____

_____

_____

_____

_____

_____

_____

_____

_____

_____

_____

The Son of Man

MATTHEW 24:36–51

Get to work, bro. Now that you're a Christian, you need to be busily at work doing the will of God by (after baptism) joining and contributing to a church, evangelizing, seeing the evangelized evangelize, and keeping global missions on your heart. We need to be busily at work because we don't know when Jesus is coming back! Remembering that "the Son of Man" refers to Jesus. *Read Matthew 24:36–44.*

This is one of those mesmerizing, yet unsettling passages that teaches us about the rapture. The Second Coming of Jesus is one of the climactic moments in the end times when Jesus will return to this world at an unexpected instant. It is unexpected by design. Because we can't know when it will happen, we are forced to do the will of God as though it could be any second. It could happen before you . . . finish . . . this . . . sentence. Okay, well, it may not have happened in that sentence, but it could happen . . . in this one? Nope? Okay. Well, one thing's for sure and always true in this earthly life: it's closer now than ever. Write that on your Matt Marker now. *Then, read Matthew 24:45–51.*

Write "it's closer now than ever" here on this page.

Integrity and Self-Control

ACTS 24:22–27

Did you write "the Second Coming of Jesus is closer than ever" on your Matt Marker? If not, write it on your Acts Axe. Jesus' imminent (constantly possible) return motivates me to share the gospel here and around the world. The fact that people are lost and will spend eternity in hell apart from God motivates everything I do with my life. Speaking of mission trips, let's check in on Paul and his mission trip in *today's Scripture*.

Felix was hoping that Paul would bribe him, but Paul chose to keep his integrity even though it kept him in prison for over two years! What a testimony. Now, did you see that Paul's biblical teachings on righteousness and self-control freaked Felix out (verse 25)? Being a Christian with self-control, a fruit of the Holy Spirit according to Galatians 5, will make some people uncomfortable. They'll try to change you even though doing so won't change God's standards. They won't hear you out because they prefer their own lostness and sin to the light of the gospel (John 3:19), but you are to press on and endure!

Does your faith make others uncomfortable? Why or why not?

Love

1 JOHN 2:1–11

Now that you're a Christian, you're to be all about love. See distant nations full of lost people through the lens of love. According to today's text, Jesus died as the propitiation (substitute) not just for your sins, but for the sins of the whole world (verse 2)! As we saw on Day 83, all the commands of the Bible come down to this call to love. Here's that call again in *today's Scripture.*

Remember that the partial purpose of 1 John, among other books, was to counter a false teaching of Gnosticism that was rising in the church. The Gnostic Christians claimed to have been given special knowledge from God. They hated the dual nature of Jesus as both God (spirit) and man (physical). So, they wrote these false gospels under the names of people like Judas, Philip, and Mary. Even an anti-Christian historian will tell you that these books were written centuries after Judas, Philip, Mary, and the other Gnostic gospels' claimed authors died. Today, you need to remember verse 2 and be righteously skeptical of any Gnostic-style teaching that contradicts it. Remember that God loves the world and don't be persuaded of anything else.

What did you learn from today's Scripture?

Talent

MATTHEW 25:14–30

Remembering that the word *talent* referred to a form of legal tender or currency like a dollar. *Read today's Scripture.* This text tells us to get to work with what God has given us, and it teaches us something incredible about heaven. It paints a picture of believers standing before God at the end of their days and God eternally rewarding those who did His will. Then, there's this guy who didn't do anything. He didn't do God's will, showing himself to be a Matthew 7 "Christian" who never knew God at all.

This passage makes me excited about heaven and it motivates me while I'm on Earth. Now that you're a Christian, you're heading toward heaven! That's amazing! Now, get to work. Get to work with the spiritual gifts you've been given. Not everyone will have "five talents" like Paul. Some of us are "two talent" Christians, but even Christians of honorably modest spiritual fruit still share in God's happiness and that is truly admirable!

Which of your talents can God use?

Global Missions

ACTS 26:24–32

Right now, as I sit at my desk with my son Cozy in my lap and look out at the palm trees, I'm praying that God would place a love in your heart for global missions; that you would be called one day to go overseas and reach someone on some distant shore who needs to hear the gospel. *Read today's Scripture.*

Paul is speaking to King Agrippa here and is trying to convince him to become a Christian, but Agrippa is being really stubborn about it (verse 28). Though he's been unjustly chained for years at this point, Paul still just wants his captors to be saved (verse 29). He will stop at nothing to bring people to faith in Christ. May you aspire to be like Paul. Even though you get shot down over and over in evangelism, may you never cease to obey the Great Commission. You never know. A guy I shared my faith with repeatedly, with no results for our whole childhood, recently called me and asked me to be the officiant (minister) for his wedding. So, like Paul, press on no matter what as you evangelize. Like Paul, go on global mission one day.

Where in the world would you like to go and share the gospel?

Revelation

REVELATION 1:1–20

Okay, Cozy's out of my lap and now Asher the Basher is "helping" me write. The book of Revelation is the one book of the Bible that promises a blessing to whomever reads and heeds it (verse 3). Cool huh? Now that you're a Christian, you need to be disciplined, focused, and unafraid of studying big beefy passages of the Bible. That shouldn't be too hard. Look at all you've already read! *Read today's Scripture.*

Of course, one captivating theme of this chapter is Christ's return. The other theme, though, introduces the focus of Revelation's first four chapters. Here, Jesus is walking among the lampstands that represent seven different churches and, by application of the Bible, our churches today too. Picture it. See Jesus walking through this court of lampstands looking at them in affectionate admiration and instructing them in raw and perfect confrontation. The Holy Spirit is in your church. Did you know that? Like these seven churches, your church may have some deep flaws, but it's still the bride of Christ. It still matters to God and the church as a whole still stands under the prophesied victory of Matthew 16:18—that the gates of hell cannot overcome it.

Can you imagine Christ's return? Write down your thoughts.

Sacrifice

MATTHEW 26:6–13

Jesus is going to make a prophecy in this, our final passage from the gospel of Matthew in a study that has spanned these two combined devotional books. Before getting up from your desk chair or hovercraft captain's chair (whichever), you'll see that prophecy fulfilled. By the way, stop reading while driving a hovercraft: it's dangerous. *Read today's Scripture.*

In verse 13, Jesus prophesied that this event would be proclaimed throughout the world and you, having just read it from history's best-selling book, saw that prophecy fulfilled the moment you read it. Jesus knew that the crucifixion, which we studied in *What It Means to Be a Christian*, is coming soon and this beautiful worship offering was, perhaps without the woman realizing it, a preparation for Jesus' burial (verse 12). The perfume was worth a whole year's wages (Mark 14:5). It was incredibly valuable and *that's what made it a worshipful sacrifice.* She poured it out, which proves that she never intended to get it back. *That* is worship. Let your whole life be a sacrifice of praise to God (Romans 12:1–2). Don't give only what you can afford to lose. Don't expect to receive it back.

What new gift can you offer to God?

Shot Down

ACTS 28:7–31

If you've loved this survey of the book of Acts, you'll love the series within *365 Devos for Teen Guys* in which we highlight the miracles of the book of Acts and study the shipwreck of chapter 27. *Read today's Scripture.*

I just turned twenty-nine. For twenty-three years I've been a Christian and in that time I've led several people to Christ, but I've been shot down way more often than I've seen evangelistic fruit. That's part of the story in today's passage. In verses 7–10, Paul performs a healing miracle and, as word spreads, people come to him for healing. The beautiful thing about verses 30–31 is that they're sort of the same thing: people hearing about Paul's ministry and coming to him for healing through the gospel. After verse 31, the Holy Spirit continued to move through the history of the world and the church until it arrived right there where you sit right now. Make it your life's call to live out and, in a way, write the 29th chapter of Acts!

Who have you shared your faith with? Were you shot down, or did they accept?

_____

_____

_____

_____

_____

_____

_____

_____

_____

_____

_____

_____

_____

_____

You Made It!

REVELATION 21:1–27

Read *today's Scripture*. Wow, how amazing, right? Heaven is a perfect place where everything is new, God's presence is our source of light, and sadness is no more! Now that you're a Christian, *you're going to see that place!* If I don't get to meet you on Earth, I'll meet you in heaven.

Go back to that mirror we've used before in authentic prayer. Now that you've been baptized, now that you're an active and contributing member of your church, now that you've experienced the Holy Spirit, now that you've evangelized, now that you've seen the evangelized evangelize, and now that you have global missions on your heart, say to your reflection in a full knowledge of all that God has done, "I'm a Christian—now what? Now this (pointing at yourself). Now more (pointing to your door)." I'm so absurdly proud of you, my student!

Write down on this page: "I'm a Christian."
Believe it. Live it. Share it.